Academic IELTS

Task 1 Writing

A self-study reference and practice book with answers

IELTSedits

Academic IELTS

Task 1 Writing

A self-study reference and practice book with answers

All rights reserved

Copyright © 2016 by IELTSedits

No part of this book may be reproduced or transmitted in any form or by any means, electronic or mechanical, including photocopying, recording or by any information storage and retrieval system, without the written permission of the publisher, except where permitted by law.

ISBN: 978-0-9933668-2-6

For further information e-mail the IELTSedits team at:

IELTSedits@gmail.com

Visit our website for FREE IELTS material - www.ieltsedits.com

The IELTSedits Team

The IELTSedits team - the authors of **Academic Word List in Use** - are also able to help IELTS students wanting to further improve not only their vocabulary. but other IELTS exam skills.

ONLINE SERVICE

Improve your IELTS Writing with our online service

We offer online help for students studying IELTS writing and specialize in Writing Task 1 and Task 2 (Academic and General).

We edit every assignment, grade the tasks according to the 4 criteria the IELTS examiner uses, and offer tips to improve next time.

ONE FREE EDIT - with proof of purchase of any IELTSedits book

For more information come and visit our website at - **www.ieltsedits.com**

Or write to the IELTSedits team at - **ieltsedits@gmail.com**

Contents

	Page
Task 1 writing - different types	1
Writing an introduction	2 - 3
Writing an overview	4 - 5
Writing a main body	6 - 7
Prepositions	8
Becoming a flexible writer	9 - 10
Degree of change - Speed of change	11
Extra Practice	12
Figures	13 - 15
Analyzing - time period	16 - 22
Analyzing - no time period	23 - 30
Diagrams in the future	31
Common errors	32
Cycles, processes, flow charts, maps,	33 - 34
Cycles	35 - 36
Processes	37 - 38
Flow charts	39 - 40
Maps	41 - 45
ANSWERS	47 - 51

♦ Task 1 Writing - different types ♦

The IELTS writing test consists of two parts - Task 1 and Task 2 - which must be completed within 60 minutes.

Task 1 is a report about a diagram such as a bar chart or table that should take about 20 minutes to write.

Task 2 is an essay about a topic of global concern such as global warming or the effects of tourism on a country and should take about 40 minutes.

Task 1 is actually easier than Task 2 but students often find it harder and spend more time writing Task 1 than Task 2. This is not a problem if you finish both tasks. Finish means that you must have written at least the minimum number of words for Task 1 - 150 words and Task 2 - 250 words. However, it is important to realise that when the IELTS examiner decides your grade, Task 2 is more valuable than Task 1. For instance:

Task 1 Grade	Task 2 Grade	Final Writing Grade
6	5	**5**
5	6	**6**

The aim of this book is to help you write Task 1 more easily and more quickly. Completing it in 20 minutes or less is certainly possible and is a target you should aim for. While speed is important, you will also be introduced to the best vocabulary and phrases to use for each paragraph - Introduction - Overview - Main Body - and shown the common grammar mistakes that many students make.

♦ Types of Diagrams ♦

There are many different types of diagram. This can make it seem as if there are too many things to learn and often discourages the student. However, any of these could be in your IELTS exam and so you need to study them all. They are:

bar charts / line charts / pie charts / tables

cycles / processes / flow charts / maps

These can be taught in two stages with the first listed group taught first and the second listed group taught second. This is because there are obvious connections with in each group and this allows us to write each group in a particular style.

♦ Writing an introduction ♦

The first thing to know is that the Task 1 introduction provided in your IELTS test can be improved. What the examiner is looking for is to see if you have added extra information and can paraphrase some of the original introduction.

♦ Adding extra information ♦

The information you need to add can change from diagram to diagram but it is possible to generalise and use a check-list of items that you must look for every time you are writing an introduction. Look at the introduction that follows the table below and list the different types of information it contains.

	2000		2005	
	Share of Global Consumption in per cent	Consumption Per Person in liters	Share of Global Consumption in per cent	Consumption Per Person in liters
United States	16.5	61.6	17.4	99.2
China	5.5	4.7	7.8	9.9
Indonesia	4.0	20.2	4.6	33.3
Italy	8.5	160.4	6.8	191.9
Germany	7.8	101.8	6.4	128.4
France	6.9	126.2	5.1	139.1
India	2.0	2.1	3.8	5.6

Example:
The table provides data on the consumption of water in seven countries over a 6-year period from 2000 to 2005.

Useful information to add to your introduction:

1. the type of chart - **The table**
2. what is being compared - **consumption of water**
3. the number of categories - **seven countries**
4. time period - **a 6-year period**
5. years - **2000 to 2005**

You can always look for this information when writing an introduction and try to paraphrase any information that is already in the original Task 1 introduction.

♦ **Writing an introduction** ♦

Introductions with all of the relevant information usually work out at between 20 - 30 words in length. Diagrams with no time period will usually have shorter introductions than diagrams with a time period.

♦ **Useful phrases for your introduction** ♦

Useful phrases to begin and end the sentence are:

The table presents data on	
The bar charts present information on	Notice that the verb has no - s - here
over a 3-year period from 2000 to 2002.	You must count ALL the years - 2000, 2001, 2002
The line chart and table provide data on	

Exercise
Look at these introductions and decide if anything needs to be changed.

1. The pie chart presented below shows data on the number of miles travelled by 5 types of transport in 7 different countries.

2. The two tables presents information on the number of crimes per 5 different age groups in 4 cities in Europe over a 3-year period form 2003 to 2006.

3. The line chart shows that the number of students attending 3 different schools over a 10- year period from 2000 to 2010.

4. The bar chart presents data on the rising people in 6 countries over a 50-year period from 1960 - 2010.

Exercise
Now look at these other Task 1 examples and write the introductions by using the information provided.

1. 1996 to 1999 / Brazil, Peru, Colombia / number of people in prison for drugs / table

2. 12-21 / 22-35 /36-55 / 55 plus / bar chart / 5 radio stations / number of listeners

3. pie chart / 8 consumer products / 5 cities in Europe / annual sales / 2005 to 2016

♦ Writing an overview - time period ♦

The second paragraph is the overview and should be about 20-25 words in length. It gives an overview of the diagram but must not include any figures from the main body. As you have decided to write an overview you DO NOT need to write a conclusion.

A very typical thing to look for when there is a time period would be a trend. This states what has happened to the figures over the whole time period. Yes, it is possible to write more clearly about how the figures have fluctuated and to state how the figures have increased at a certain time and then fallen and so on but this is too much information. Also, simply stating that the figures have fluctuated is NOT a good overview.

♦ Useful phrases for your overview ♦

Useful phrases to begin the sentence are:

The overall trend shows that	
Overall,	sales for all three categories fell over this period of time.
An overview of the diagram shows that	
Over this period of time,	sales for New York and Boston rose whereas figures for Ohio fell.

Exercise

Look at the line chart below and write the introduction and overview about car sales by two companies - x and y.

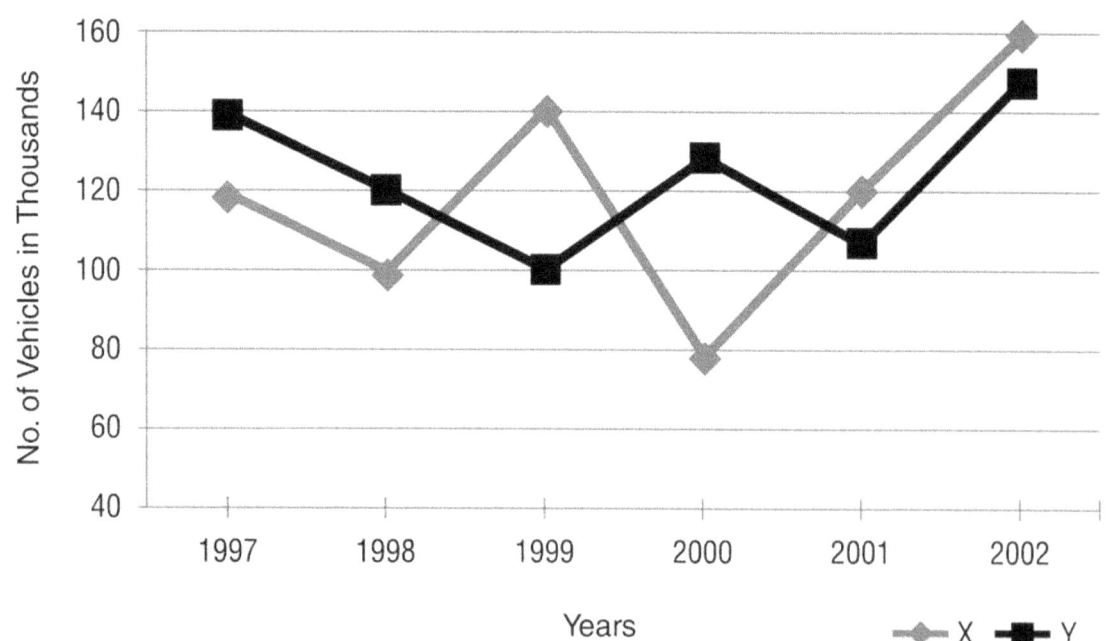

♦ Writing a - no time period - overview ♦

It is important to be able to recognise when your diagram has a time period and when it does not. This is not difficult to do but is something you must notice before you start writing. Remember that your skill in writing is judged not just on grammar and spelling but whether or not the information you include is correct.

It should be clear that you cannot write about trends when there is no time period. So, you need to look at something else to write about. The easiest way is to write about the biggest and (possibly) the smallest figure.

Look at the diagram below and decide what information you want to add to your overview. The table shows the percentage of promotional offers for various food products.

	Wegmans	Publix	Costco	Fareway
Food Categories	%	%	%	%
Fruit and vegetables	12	14	16	17
Fatty and sugary foods	27	37	33	35
Other foods	62	46	52	51

♦ Useful phrases for your Overview ♦

Useful phrases to begin the sentence are:

Overall,
An overview of the diagram shows that

there were more promotions for other foods than for the other three categories.

Notice that you could have focused on the supermarkets with the biggest percentage of promotional offers and this would have led to an overview like this:

Overall, Wegmans had the highest percentage of goods being promoted for other foods whereas the largest for fatty and sugary foods, and fruit and vegetables were Publix and Fareway respectively.

♦ Writing a Main Body ♦

When writing a main body it is important to use the correct verb tense. It is very common for students to write, phrases like - **sales have increased to**, **sales have been increased to**, and **sales were increased to**.

It is much easier and quicker to use the simple past and as most of the charts show information from the past it makes sense to do this. If no date is given, you could use the simple present but the simple past is still correct to use.

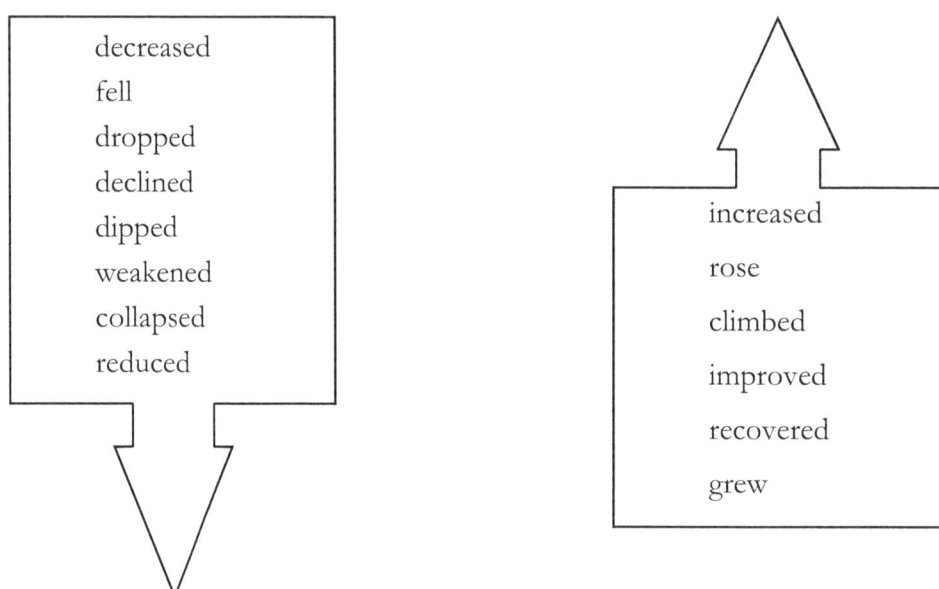

N.B.
Avoid using the words **DOWN** or **UP** as these are too informal for this style of writing. So, phrases like - **sales went up** and **sales went down** should not be used.

♦ Common prepositions to use with verbs ♦

A lot of different prepositions can be used but by far the most common ones are shown here..

TO / FROM / IN / BY

1. Literacy levels **in** Malaysia **rose to** 98.5% **in** 2011 **from** 65.2% **in** 1953.

2. Unemployment levels **dropped in** Germany **from** 9.8% **in** 1976 **to** 7.5% **in** 2009.

3. The number of students attending Roman History **increased by** 27 students, **improving from** 12 students **in** 2008 to 39 **in** 2012.

♦ Writing a Main Body ♦

While earlier on we focused on how to describe actual changes that happen in a diagram, it is also important to realise that sometimes figures - even in a diagram with a time period - stay the same. These are also important parts of the diagram and can be expressed using the phrases shown below. Again, the simple past is being used.

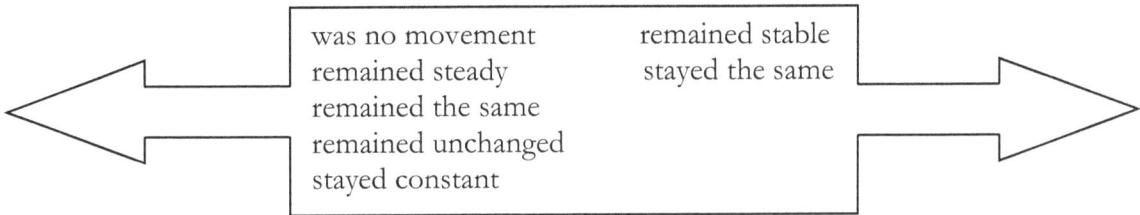

♦ Useful prepositions for periods of No Change ♦

AT / FROM

Average property prices in Hong Kong **remained the same** for a two-bedroom flat **at** US$ 35,000 over three consecutive years **from** 1997 to 1999.

Although France experienced the largest continued rise in perfume sales **from** US$1.7 million in 2003 to US$ 2.9 million in 2007, there was **no movement** in sales **from** 2007 to 2009 when figures **remained the same at** US$ 3.2 million.

Exercise

Use the words and phrases in the box to complete the report that follows about attendance at the Nelsonville Music Festival.

More specifically, the longest continued ———— in festival goers was from 1976 to 1988 where figures ———— from a little under 250 to exactly 4,000; an ———— of just over 3,750 over 13 years. This figure was not attained again for 19 years when ———— people went to the Nelsonville Music Festival in 2006 with a total of slightly more than 4,000, more visitors than at any other time. This was an obvious contrast to 1976, the ———— over this time. One further point to note is that attendance ———— at exactly 3,000 over 3-consecutive years from 1996 to 1998. After the continued ———— to 1988, attendance bottomed out in 1992 and 1994 with a little over 2,500 in both years.

> increase
>
> lowest attendance
>
> more
>
> remained the same
>
> rise
>
> rose
>
> climb

7

♦ Main Body ♦

♦ Preposition Exercises ♦

Exercise

Complete the Task 1 report that follows by adding the necessary prepositions in the report about the relative importance of 10 environmental problems.

> at (2x)   for (3x)   from
> in (2x)   of (3x)
> to (2x)   over

The bar chart compares and contrasts the changes ——— the importance ——— 10 environmental issues faced by America ——— a 4-year period from 2003 to 2006.

Overall, although the majority ——— these problems became less important over this period of time, awareness ——— the need to address global warming rose dramatically.

More specifically, the biggest change ——— importance was ——— the issue of global warming, rising ——— a little over 20% ——— just under 50%. Acid rain stayed ——— 10th place with a little under 25% in both years. Both overpopulation and ozone depletion remained unchanged ——— a little under 25.0% and 22.5% respectively. The biggest reversal in importance was ——— water pollution which was the most important environmental problem in 2003 with a little under 40%; figures fell ——— slightly under 15% to just over 25%. This compared with views ——— toxic waste which dropped from a little over 30% to a little under 22.5%.

8

♦ Writing a Main Body ♦

♦ Becoming a flexible writer ♦

One part of writing a good assignment - and this is true for both Task 1 and Task 2 - is showing the IELTS examiner that your writing can be flexible. This means that you are able to write the same information, or similar information, in a different way using different sentence structures.

This is particularly important when rewriting the introductions of Task 1 and Task 2 and writing a conclusion in Task 2 as this is a summary of the main body paragraphs.

Look at this sample of a main body and see if you like it.

> The cost of health insurance rose from US$12 per month in 1995 to US$15 per month in 2000. Following this the cost was US$16 per month in 2001, 2002, 2003, 2004, 2005 and 2006. Finally, the cost of insurance rose from US$16 in 2006 to US$19 in 2009.

This sample of a main body might look good - it certainly reads well - but it is wrong for a number of different reasons.

1. The sentence structures are very similar - see sentences 1 and 3.

2. Nothing has been shown as important. If it is not important why write about it?

3. Lists are often best avoided and so - 2001, 2002, 2003, 2004, 2005 and 2006 would be seen by the examiner as not concise enough.

4. It would have been better to have avoided repeating the word - **rose** - by using a synonym. This is easily done and much more impressive for the examiner

A better example (with only slight changes) would be:

> The cost of health insurance **rose** from **its lowest point of** US$12 per month in 1995 to US$15 per month in 2000. Following this the cost **remained the same** from 2001 to 2006 at US$16 per month. Finally, the cost of insurance **increased** from US$16 in 2006 to **its highest point of** US$19 in 2009.

This example is much better and has helped increase the grade for Task Achievement. The sentence structure for sentences 1 and 3 are still very similar but this will be looked at in the next few pages. Notice how each sentence has been made important by adding a few extra words.

        its lowest point   remained the same   its highest point

♦ Writing a Main Body ♦

♦ Becoming a flexible writer ♦

Common main body sentences are:

1. Income tax **increased in** Seoul from 5% in 1995 to **a peak of** 9% in 2005.

2. Overall NHS funding per capita **increased by** 75% between 1990 with 21% and 2004, **the highest figure in the chart**, with 96%.

These are very good sentences that show why the figures are important and can be used in a main body. The examiner, however, also looks for a variety of sentence patterns. This can be done by turning the verb into a noun and changing the start of the sentence. For example:

NOUNS - IN / OF

1. There was **an increase in** income tax in Seoul from 5% in 1995 to **a peak of** 9% in 2005.

2. There was **an increase of** 75 per cent in overall NHS funding per capita between 1990 with 21% and 2004, **the highest figure in the chart**, with 96%.

Notice that the preposition sometimes has to change when you convert the verb to a noun. Look at sentence 2 where it changes from - **increased by 75%** - to - **an increase of 75%**.

The preposition in sentence 1 stayed the same but was used in a different way - **Income tax increased in Seoul - There was an increase in income tax in Seoul.**

Exercise
Complete the tables below to complete the list of verbs and nouns.

Verb	Noun	Verb	Noun
decreased	a decrease	increased	an increase
fell		rose	
dropped		climbed	
declined		improved	
dipped		recovered	
reduced		grew	
weakened			

♦ Writing a Main Body ♦

♦ Degree of change / Speed of change ♦

As you can now see, it is possible to change the order of information - **nouns and verbs** - in order to rewrite your sentences. Further changes can be made by referring more directly to how quickly or how much the figures changed.

Exercise
Complete the sentences below by choosing the correct answer from the words in italics.

1. Fuel consumption ………. from 120 litres in 2006 to 360 litres in 2007, a 3-fold rise.
   dramatic rise / rose dramatically
2. There was ………. in average temperature between 1975 and 2005 of 0.3C.
   a slight drop / dropped slightly
3. Bakers experienced a steady ………. in salary over 6-consecutive years (1963 - 1968) of 10% per year.
   rose / rising / rise
4. The number of online students ………. from an initial 5 students in March to 130 in December.
   increased / an increase / increasing
5. The recycling program resulted in a ………. in the amount of paper recycled, 600kg to 1,200kg.
   double climbing / 2-fold climb / double

N.B.
The ideas in sentence 1 and 5 can be used a lot when developing ideas for the main body.

1. The price of chocolate rose from US$2.50 in 1967 to US$5.00 in 1980; **a 2-fold rise**

2. Shares climbed rapidly over the first 6 months 0f 2015 from US$1.50 a share to US$10 a share; **a 10-fold climb**

3. Flight tickets to Japan **doubled** from 650 Yen in 2005 to 1,300 Yen in 2007.

♦ **Writing a Main Body** ♦

♦ **Extra Practice** ♦

Exercise
Look at the following sentences and pick the correct form to complete each sentence.

1. In 1995, Australian —- **exports / exporting** —- to South East Asia were slightly less than 30% of exports.

2. The early 80s witnessed a substantial —- **dropped / drop** —- to 500 million.

3. After 1999, there was a gradual —- **fall / fallen** —- to nearly 73 minutes in 2002, and as a result, the number of minutes of a local call in 2002 was equal to that of 1995.

4. In Italy, the ratio will show a —- **dramatic / dramatically** —- increase —- **from / by** —- 24.1% to 42.3%.

5. Theme parks received less than 400 thousand guests, and the sports events had —- **slightly / slight** —- less than 200 thousand.

6. The percentage of people possessing computers saw a —- **gradually / gradual** —- **increased / increase** —- from less than 60 percent to more than 70 percent in 2010.

7. By the year 2005, gas usage experienced an —- **increased / increase** —- from 29.63% to 30.31% whereas the extraction of petro plunged —- **significant / significantly** —- to only 19.55%.

8. In the following period between 1989 and 1993, the number of women killed by the disease —- **remained / remaining** —- unchanged at just over 480.

9. The number of texts used was largest in the under 18 group, at —- **slight / slightly** —- under 3,000.

10. The suburban areas suffered the —- **sharpest / sharp** —- climb in growth rate among the three areas, and jumped to 8% from 2%.

N.B. All of these sentences are adapted from those written by students and so might be missing some of the features that make a sentence worthy of a higher grade.

♦ Writing a Main Body ♦

♦ Figures ♦

As you have already seen, **it is essential** to state why figures are important. For example:

The **highest taxes** over this period of time were in Singapore with the **highest figure** in 2010.

However, if sentences like this continued it would result in a grade of around 5.0 for Task Achievement because there are no figures.

♦ Adding figures to the Main Body ♦

To write a good main body sentence you need to:
1. **explain why certain figures are important**
2. **make sure that you add the figures**.

Exercise
Look at the bar chart below and decide what parts of this are important.

The sales of books (in thousands) from six branches of a publishing company during two consecutive years 2000 and 2001.

Also, for extra practice, try to write an introduction and overview.

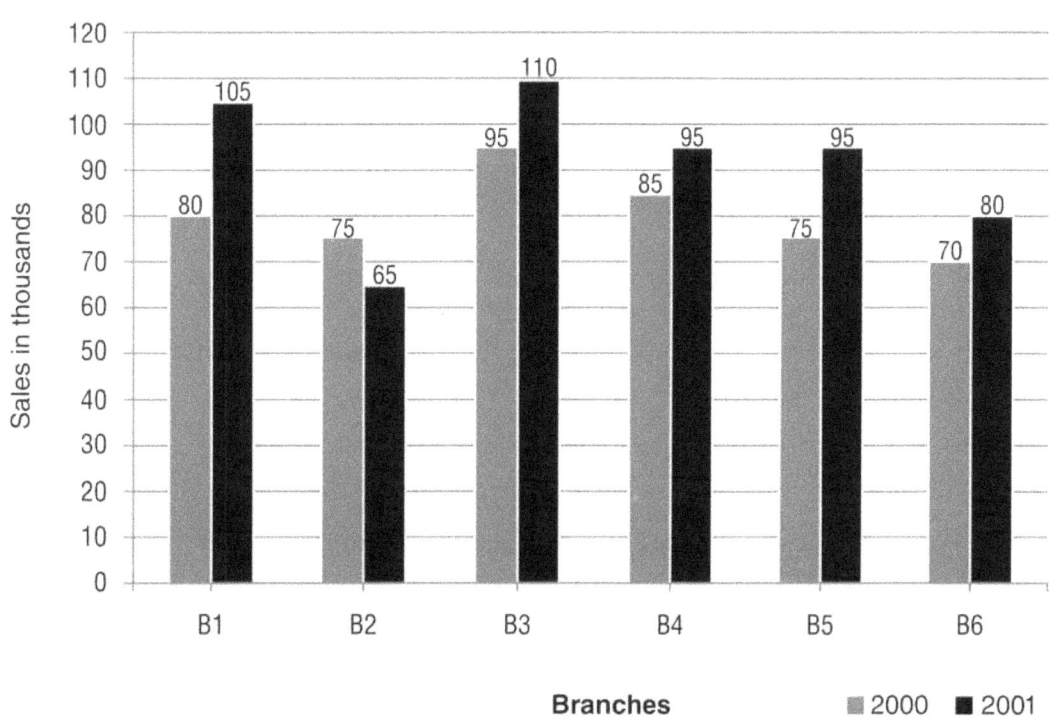

♦ **Writing a Main Body** ♦

♦ **Figures** ♦

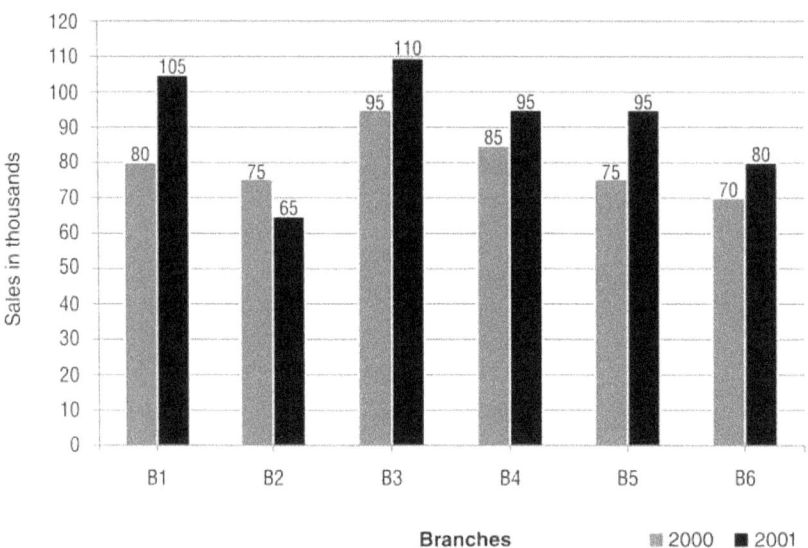

Here there is no excuse for not presenting accurate figures as they are all stated clearly in the chart. Even here, some students still write things like -

WRONG - The number of books sold in 2001 in branch B1 was **105**..

CORRECT - The number of books sold in 2001 in branch B1 was **105,000**..
(Remember to use the units)

WRONG - The number of books sold in 2001 in B2 was **roughly 65,000**.

CORRECT - The number of books sold in 2001 in B2 was **exactly 65,000**.
(Avoid saying - **roughly** - when you know **exactly** what the figures are.)

Here are a few sentences you might have written using this chart.

1. The biggest increase over these two years was in B1 where sales increased from 80,000 books in 2000 to 105,000 in 2001.

2. The only branch to experience a decrease in sales was B2 where sales fell from 75,000 to 65,000; a drop of 10,000 books.

3. Branches B4 and B5 had exactly the same number of sales in 2001 with 95,000 books; this was the same figures as in B3 in 2000.

4. Branch B3 had the highest sales in both 2000 and 2001 with 95,000 and 110,000 respectively.

♦ Writing a Main Body ♦

♦ Figures must be accurate ♦

Some diagrams - tables and pie charts - are very easy to interpret because the exact figures are given but line charts and bar charts might not always be so user friendly. You need to spend a little time deciding what the figures are. Some useful phrases that will help you write sentences and impress the IELTS examiner are shown below.

| a little more than |
| just over |
| slightly above |

| a little less than |
| just under |
| slightly below |

Exercise
Look at the line chart and try to estimate some of the figures using phrases from the table above. Try to focus on figures which are important.

Exercise
Also, for extra practice, try to write an introduction, overview and main body..

The number of earthquakes experienced in one region of the world.

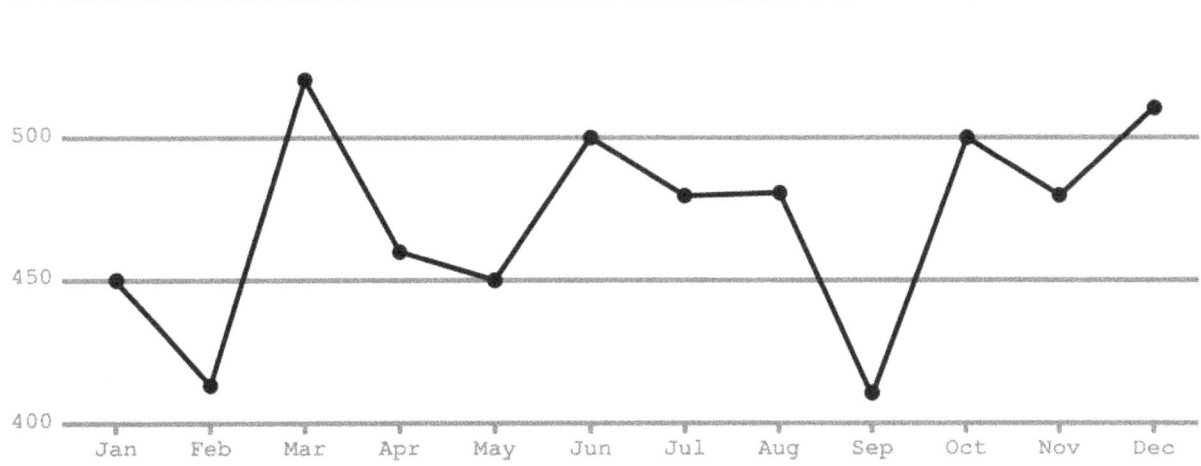

♦ **Writing a Main Body** ♦

♦ **Analyzing - time period diagrams** ♦

The number of earthquakes experienced in one region of the world.

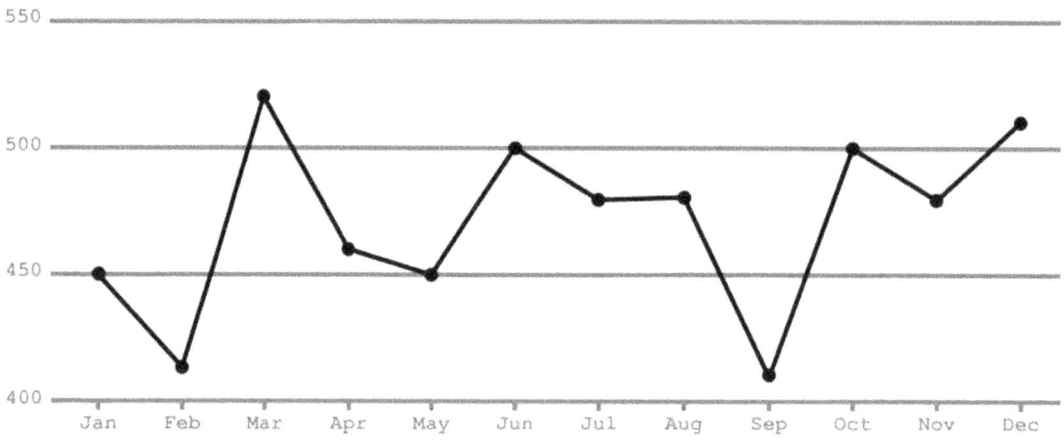

1. The **largest number** of earthquakes occurred in March with slightly less than 525 compared with just over 400, **the smallest number**, in September.

2. **No change** in the frequency of earthquakes happened in two consecutive months, July and August, when a little over 475 happened in both months.

3. Some months had the **same number** of earthquakes with January and May having exactly 450 earthquakes and June and October 500.

4. The **biggest rise** in the number of earthquakes over two consecutive months was from February to March with figures rising from a little under 425 to just under 525.

5. Over these twelve months **the difference between** the number of earthquakes in January (450) and those in December (just over 510) was a little over 60..

N.B. Remember that while using brackets is a good way to present figures - it's easy - the examiner does not want to see all of the figures present in this way. The main reason for this is that by using brackets you do not need prepositions and so the sentence structure is less impressive.

♦ Writing a Main Body ♦

♦ Analyzing - time period diagrams ♦

A diagram with a time period is much easier to analyze because there are many more things to look for than when writing a main body for a diagram with no time period. However, many students still try to analyze by looking at the diagram with no clear objective in mind.

This often results in a main body that is just describing the figures with no reason why each sentence is important.

What the examiner is looking for, however, are sentences like this:

The **largest figure** for child labour was in Mexico with approximately 12% of children between the ages of 5 and 14 working.

The **lowest figure** for people watching television was in the over 60s group with only 8%.

Exercise
Look at the table below and try to find some important features to write about. Use the fact that things change as a big hint for what to look for.

Worldwide Mobile Phone Sales in 2005 and 2006 (% share of market)

Company	2005 % Market Share	2006 % Market Share
Nokia	32.5	35
Motorola	17.7	21.1
Samsung	12.7	11.8
Sony Ericsson	6.3	7.4
L.G.	6.7	6.3
BenQ Mobile	4.9	2.4
Others	19.2	16.2
TOTAL	100.0	100.0

Exercise
For extra practice also write the introduction and overview.

♦ **Writing a Main Body** ♦

♦ **Analyzing - time period diagrams** ♦

Worldwide Mobile Phone Sales in 2005 and 2006 (% share of market)

Company	2005 % Market Share	2006 % Market Share
Nokia	32.5	35
Motorola	17.7	21.1
Samsung	12.7	11.8
Sony Ericsson	6.3	7.4
L.G.	6.7	6.3
BenQ Mobile	4.9	2.4
Others	19.2	16.2
TOTAL	100.0	100.0

1. **More Nokia phones** were sold in 2005 and 2006 than any other phone with 32.5% and 35% respectively.

2. By contrast, **the fewest number** of phones were sold by BenQ Mobile with 4.9% and 2.4% sold in 2005 and 2006 respectively.

3. **Both** Sony Ericsson and L.G. captured 6.3% of the market in 2005 and 2006 respectively.

4. The **smallest increase in market share** over these two years happened with Sony Ericsson rising slightly from 6.3% to 7.4%; a rise of only 1.1%.

5. The **second largest percentage** in 2005 was other brands gaining 19.2% of the market but this ranking was then taken by Motorola in 2006 with 21.1%.

♦ **Writing a Main Body** ♦

♦ **Analyzing - time period diagrams** ♦

Exercise

Look at the table below and try to find some important features to write about. Use ideas from the previous examples to help you develop your ideas.

Percentage of students giving good ratings for different aspects of a university

	2000	2005	2010
Technical Quality	65	63	69
Print Resources	87	89	88
Electronic Resources	45	72	88
Range of modules offered	32	30	27
Building / Teaching Facilities	77	77	77

♦ **Writing a Main Body** ♦

♦ **Analyzing - time period diagrams** ♦

Percentage of students giving good ratings for different aspects of a university

	2000	2005	2010
Technical Quality	65	63	69
Print Resources	87	89	88
Electronic Resources	45	72	88
Range of modules offered	32	30	27
Building / Teaching Facilities	77	77	77

1. The **largest ratings** are always for print resources with 87% and 89% for the years 2000 and 2005 respectively and a tie with electronic resources in 2010 with 88%.

2. The **only category** to experience the **same ratings** over the whole time period was building and teaching facilities with 77% of the students selecting this.

3. The **only aspect to always rise** was electronic resources which climbed from a rating of 45% in 2000 to 88% in 2010; slightly less than a two-fold rise.

4. Of the 5 aspects, the range of modules offered **always had the lowest ratings** with 32%, 30% and 27% over the three given years.

5. **The only category** to experience **a peak** in ratings was print resources with 89% in 2005.

N.B.
Not all categories need to be capitalized even if they have capital letters in the chart. You must decide if the words being used are proper nouns and, therefore, need to be capitalized. In this chart all of the categories are not proper nouns.

♦ Writing a Main Body ♦

♦ Analyzing - time period diagrams ♦

It might come as a surprise that this table is listed as a time period diagram. Where are the years? However, the different age groups create time and show you that things do change as a person gets older.

Exercise
Look at the table below and try to find some important features to write about. Use ideas from the previous examples to help you develop your ideas.

The table below shows in which sector of the economy different age groups were employed.

Employment sector	18-25 age group	25-40 age group	40-65 age group
Agriculture	5	7	9
Manufacturing	12	15	23
Catering	6	8	4
Local government	8	12	18
Health	12	15	12
Retail	23	7	6
Law	4	4	4
Accountancy	3	2	3
Education	9	12	12
Other	21	18	9

♦ **Writing a Main Body** ♦

♦ **Analyzing - time period diagrams** ♦

The table below shows in which sector of the economy different age groups were employed.

Employment sector	18-25 age group	25-40 age group	40-65 age group
Agriculture	5	7	9
Manufacturing	12	15	23
Catering	6	8	4
Local government	8	12	18
Health	12	15	12
Retail	23	7	7
Law	4	4	4
Accountancy	3	2	3
Education	9	12	12
Other	21	18	9

1. The percentage of people working in education **remained the same** at 12% in both the 25 to 40 age group and the 40 to 65 age group.

2. Accountancy employed the **smallest percentage** of people **in all three age groups** with 3% in both the youngest and oldest age groups and 2% in those aged between 25 and 40.

3. The only category to **always decrease** was other kinds of jobs falling from 21% to 18% and then finally 9%.

4. **The only** employment sector **to remain unchanged in all three groups** was law with a percentage of 4%.

5. The **biggest overall increase** in percentage **for any of the 10 categories** was manufacturing which almost doubled from 12% in the youngest age group to 23% in the oldest group.

6. Retail at 23% in the 18-25 age group **was exactly the same as** the percentage in the oldest group but for manufacturing.

♦ Main Body ♦

♦ Analyzing - no time period diagrams ♦

Diagrams with no time period cannot use all of the vocabulary that you have seen so far. Never use verbs of change, for example - increase and decrease - or phrases that show no change over a period of time like - remained the same and period of no change.

Equally, you cannot refer to certain points of the diagram as having peaks or troughs. These can only be used with diagrams with time periods. This might leave you wondering what words or phrases you can use as there seems to be nothing left. The answer lies in the fact that your analysis of each diagram will rely only on being able to compare and contrast.

Being able to compare and contrast well is one of the key factors in writing a good main body for a diagram with no time period. It also helps with diagrams with time periods.

Exercise
Look at the table below and try to find some important features to write about. Use ideas from the previous examples to help you develop your idea

The rate of change in total deforestation when the rates of 2000-2005 and 1990-2000 are compared

Country	+ %
Malaysia	85.7
Cambodia	74.3
Burundi	47.6
Togo	41.6
Nigeria	31.1
Sri Lanka	25.4
Benin	24.1
Brazil	21.2
Uganda	21.0
Indonesia	18.6
Total change in 62 tropical countries	8.5

N.B. While very familiar words, people often get confused as to the exact meaning of compare and contrast.
Compare - things which are exactly the same or nearly the same.
Contrast - things which are very different or opposite.

♦ **Main Body** ♦

♦ **Analyzing - no time period diagrams** ♦

The rate of change in total deforestation when the rates of 2000-2005 and 1990 2000 are compared.

Country	+ %
Malaysia	85.7
Cambodia	74.3
Burundi	47.6
Togo	41.6
Nigeria	31.1
Sri Lanka	25.4
Benin	24.1
Brazil	21.2
Uganda	21.0
Indonesia	18.6
Total change in 62 tropical countries	8.5

1. The **highest rate of change** in total deforestation occurred in Malaysia with a rate of 85.7%.

2. By contrast, **the lowest rate** was in Indonesia with a rate of 18.6%; a little under 5-fold less than in Malaysia.

3. One further point to note is that the rates for Uganda and Brazil **were almost identical** at 21.0% and 21.2% respectively.

4. **The combined rates** of Togo and Nigeria add up to 72.7% and **falls slightly below** that of Cambodia which has **the second highest rate** with 74.3%.

5. **The difference in rates** between Malaysia, **the overall highest rate**, with 85.7% and **the total number of tropical countries** (8.5%) is 77.2%.

6. The countries with **the closest figures** was Uganda with 21.0% and Brazil with 21.2%; a difference of 0.2%.

♦ **Main Body** ♦

♦ **Analyzing - no time period diagrams** ♦

Exercise
Complete the sentences below by using the phrases in the box.

> occurred between   both
> the biggest difference   the most expensive
> experienced the same

1. _____ Brazil and Argentina _____ literacy levels in 2003 with 98.2%

2. _____ apartments were in Hong Kong with an average weekly cost of £ 1,750.

3. _____ in tourism _____ Thailand and Cambodia where figures were 4.5 million and 2 million respectively; a difference of 2 .5 million.

Exercise
Look at the pie chart below and try to find some important features to write about. Use ideas from the previous examples to help you develop your ideas.

The pie chart below shows the distribution of food products from Company ABC

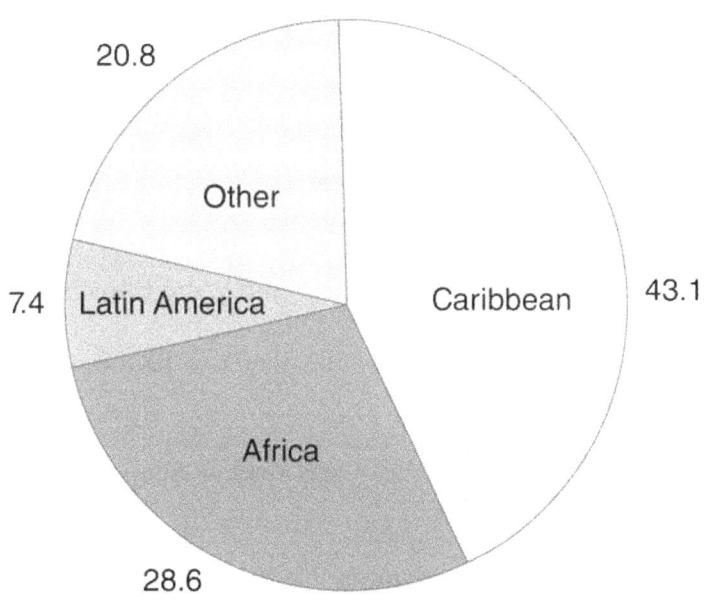

♦ **Main Body** ♦

♦ **Analyzing - no time period diagrams** ♦

The pie chart below shows the distribution of food products from Company ABC

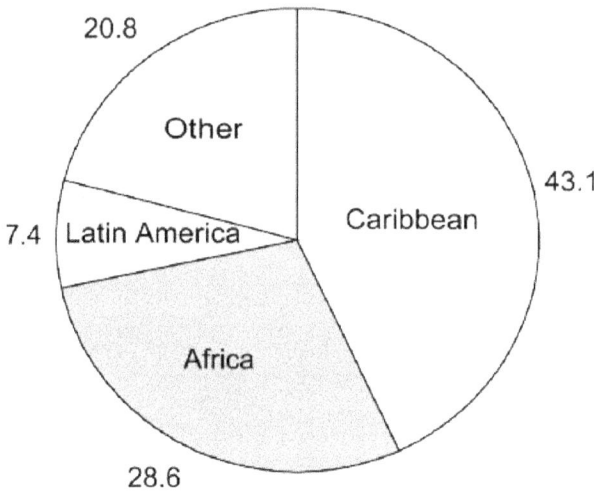

1. The Caribbean received **more food products** from Company ABC with 43.1% of the total **than any other area.**

2. **The smallest part of the market** share with 7.4% was Latin-America.

3. With **just over a quarter of the market** with 28.6% was Africa.

4. **The third biggest share** was 20.8% going to other areas of the globe.

It is very difficult to write enough for a main body with only 4 categories and 4 figures to write about but the sentences here show you that it is possible to write a list where you say things like:

        the biggest percentage / the smallest part / the third biggest share

The examiner will notice that you have varied the sentence patterns a little and this will help increase your grade.

Also, notice that you can write things like - With **just over a quarter of the market** with 28.6% was Africa.

Use fractions to help develop your ideas - **a quarter, a third, a half** - plus give the exact figure.

♦ **Main Body** ♦

♦ **Analyzing - no time period diagrams** ♦

Exercise
Look at the pie chart below and try to find some important features to write about. Use ideas from the previous examples to help you develop your ideas.

The pie chart below shows the market share of various mobile phone companies

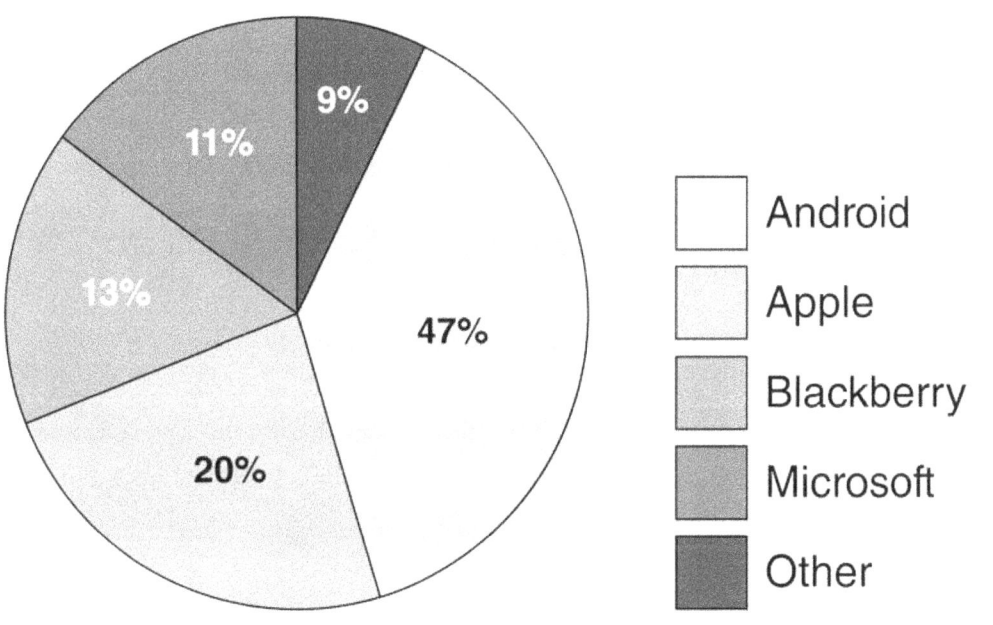

♦ **Main Body** ♦

♦ **Analyzing - no time period diagrams** ♦

The pie chart below shows the market share of various mobile phone companies

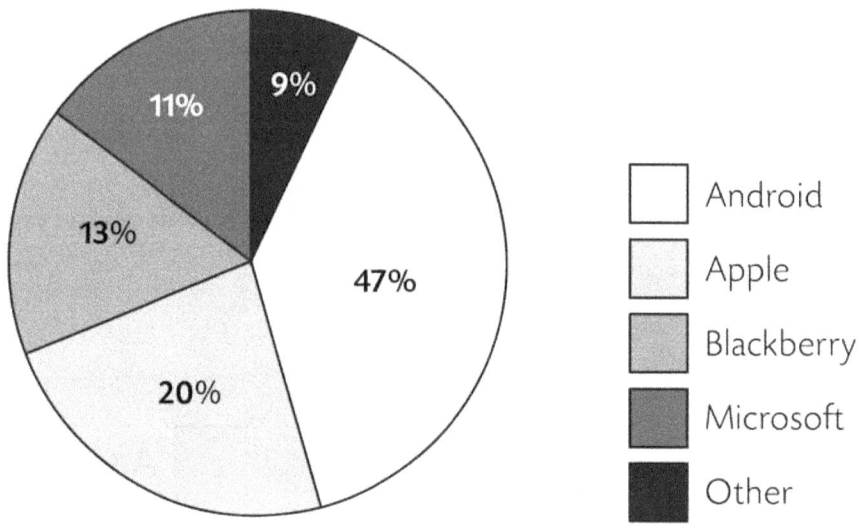

1. Android took slightly less than half of the mobile market share with 47% and was **the largest share in the group**.

2. With 20% of the market share and coming **second in the rankings** was Apple.

3. The other mobile phone category was **almost exactly a half of the market share held by Apple** having 9% of the market and Apple with 20%.

4. Both Blackberry and Microsoft attained **almost the same share of the market** with 13% and 11% respectively.

♦ **Main Body** ♦

♦ **Analyzing - no time period diagrams** ♦

Exercise
Look at the table below and try to find some important features to write about. Use ideas from the previous examples to help you develop your ideas.

The tables below show the consumption and production of potatoes in different regions in the world in 2006.

Consumption of Potatoes (Kg per person)

South and Central America	23.6
Africa	14.1
North America	57.9
Europe	96.1
Asia	25.8

Production of Potatoes (in millions of tonnes)

South and Central America	15.6
Africa	16.4
North America	24.7
Europe	126.3
Asia	131.2

♦ Main Body ♦

♦ Analyzing - no time period diagrams ♦

The tables below show the consumption and production of potatoes in different regions in the world in 2006.

Consumption of Potatoes (Kg per person)

South and Central America	23.6
Africa	14.1
North America	57.9
Europe	96.1
Asia	25.8

Production of Potatoes (in millions of tonnes)

South and Central America	15.6
Africa	16.4
North America	24.7
Europe	126.3
Asia	131.2

1. While **the highest consumption** of potatoes was in Europe with 96.1kg per person they also produced **the second highest amount** with 126.3 million tonnes.

2. **The biggest difference** in production and consumption levels was in Asia where only 25.8kg per person was eaten but 131.2 million tonnes was produced; **the largest level** of all 5 areas.

3. Consumption in Central and South America was **the second lowest** at 23.6kg and **under half the quantity eaten** in North America with 57.9kg; **the second highest**.

4. Europe produced **the second highest amount of potatoes** at 126.3 million tonnes which was **just over 5 times more** than **the third highest production levels** in North America at 24.7 million tonnes.

5. **The closest production levels** were in South and Central America and Africa where the figures were 15.6 and 16.4 million tonnes respectively: **a difference of** 0.8 million tonnes.

♦ Diagrams in the Future ♦

Diagrams with time periods usually show time in the past. However, it is possible to see a diagram where time moves into the future. The approach to writing these particular reports is very similar to the typical time period report but one point is different. For example, look at the overview below and try to find something wrong with it.

Overall, as consumption of oil increased and production remained fairly constant, oil imports rose over this period of time from 2005 to 2030.

The problem here is that this assumes that everything is in the past and so all of the changes have already happened.

♦ Useful phrases for the future ♦

Figures in the future are based on research rather than established facts and are, therefore, not certain. Whenever you mention future results you must show that the figures shown are likely but not guaranteed. This is done by using phrases such as:

> forecast
>
> expected
>
> predicted
>
> projected
>
> anticipated

Typical phrases that you can use are:

1. Sales are expected to increase from ………. to

2. An increase in sales is forecast from ……….to

3. It is predicted that sales will increase from ………. to

4. It is anticipated that sales will remain the same from ………. to ……….

♦ Common Errors ♦

While no student will write exactly what another student writes - unless they are copying - certain common errors can often been seen in a Task 1 report. Each of the errors shown here is followed by an explanation of why a mistake has been made and if necessary what should have been said.

♦ Introduction ♦

The bar chart below
You do not need to write "below" as this is not true - the diagram is **not** below

The table chart
You only need to write "table". However, you can write "pie chart"

The diagrams shows
With more than one diagram you must write "The diagrams show" - **no** "s"

The bar chart shows that
The word "that" suggests you are going to analyze the bar chart. You do that in the overview

♦ Overview ♦

Overall, hamburgers fell
Hamburgers are **not** falling. Use - "Overall, the number of hamburgers eaten fell"

The overall trend shows that, population levels in all countries went up
The word "up" is too informal so use "increased" instead

♦ Main Body ♦

The line says
The line does not say anything - instead refer to the category the line represents

The diagram shows
Do not use expressions like this in the main body. Use this for the Introduction

Figures were risen
It is better to use the simple past - "Sales rose"

Sales have risen
It is better to use the simple past - "Sales rose"

It is interesting to note
You must not use phrases like this or personal opinions in Task 1 as they are not taken directly from the diagram

♦ Cycles - Processes - Flow charts - Maps ♦

It was mentioned right at the beginning of this book that there are two main groups to study for Task 1. We have now looked at bar charts - line charts - pie charts - tables and learnt the importance of analyzing correctly.

We will now turn to the second group and look at cycles - processes - flow charts - maps. One thing that all of these diagrams have in common is change. For instance, a cycle could show how an egg changes into a frog, a process could show how a tennis racquet is made, a flow chart could show how a manager makes the decision to hire someone, and a map could show how a city has changed over the last 50 years.

♦ What structure do I use for these diagrams ? ♦

The structure for writing these diagrams is the same as for the first group of diagrams - introduction - overview - main body.

♦ What verb tense do I use ? ♦

The main verb tense to use is the **simple present** - Active or Passive.

    An Indian chef **uses** many different spices.   **Active**

    Many different spices **are used** by an Indian chef.   **Passive**

The passive form of the verb is seen as a more indirect way to give information. It focuses more on what is receiving the action (usually a thing in Task 1 IELTS) rather than the doer of the action. This style is seen as more formal and, therefore, more academic.

Active -   noun phrase **(1)** + simple present + noun phrase **(2)**

Passive -   noun phrase **(2)** + is / are + past participle (p.p.) + by + noun phrase **(1)**

N.B. The preposition - **by** - often used with the passive form can be replaced with other prepositions or phrases to explain why something is done.

Exercise
Complete the sentences below by adding the correct word or phrase from the box. More than one answer might be possible.

1. The coffee is filtered _____ separate the grains from the coffee.

2. The seeds are crushed _____ they are boiled for 10 minutes.

> before
>
> in order to

♦ **Cycles - Processes - Flow charts - Maps** ♦

♦ **What phrases can I use ?** ♦

Although these diagrams show change, no time period is given (the exception is for some maps and a few cycles). However, to show that these changes are happening over a period of time, you can use time order phrases.

First of all,

At first,

Initially,

Secondly,

Next,

Subsequently,

After completing this,

When this has been done,

Then,

After that,

Later on,

Finally,

♦ **Cycles** ♦

The Frog Cycle

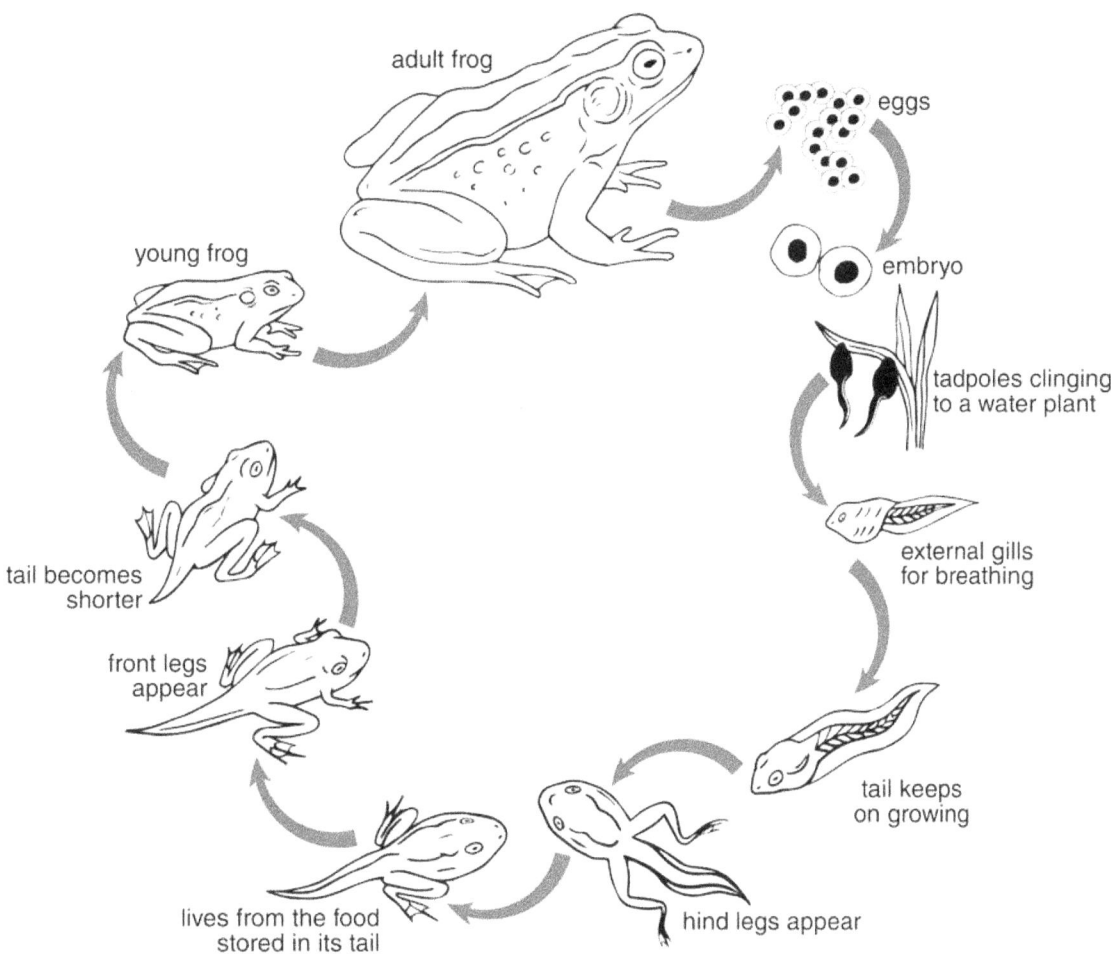

Exercise
Write an introduction, overview and main body for this cycle.

N.B. You need to decide where to start the cycle. The adult frog or egg would be a good place to start. If you start with the adult frog then your cycle must end back with the adult frog. This makes sure that you have really completed the cycle. If you start with the egg then end with the egg.

The overview can often be combined with the introduction by explaining more clearly the key parts of the cycle.

♦ Cycles ♦

You can, use the style used here for the processes and flow charts. Note that the introduction is combined with the overview.

The diagram shows the different stages needed in the completion of the frog cycle which starts with clumps of many eggs and then progresses through different forms until finally producing an adult frog.

To begin with many eggs are laid in a clump with each of them containing a small embryo. Once developed into tadpoles they leave the eggs and use water plants as protection form their environment. External gills can be seen that are used for breathing. The tail of the tadpoles keep growing and eventually the hind legs appear. At this stage the shape of the tadpoles head changes and nutrition is provided by the tail. The front legs then appear and so a small frog can be seen but still with a tail. This continues to grow shorter until eventually a young frog has developed. Once an adult frog, the female s can lay eggs to complete the cycle.

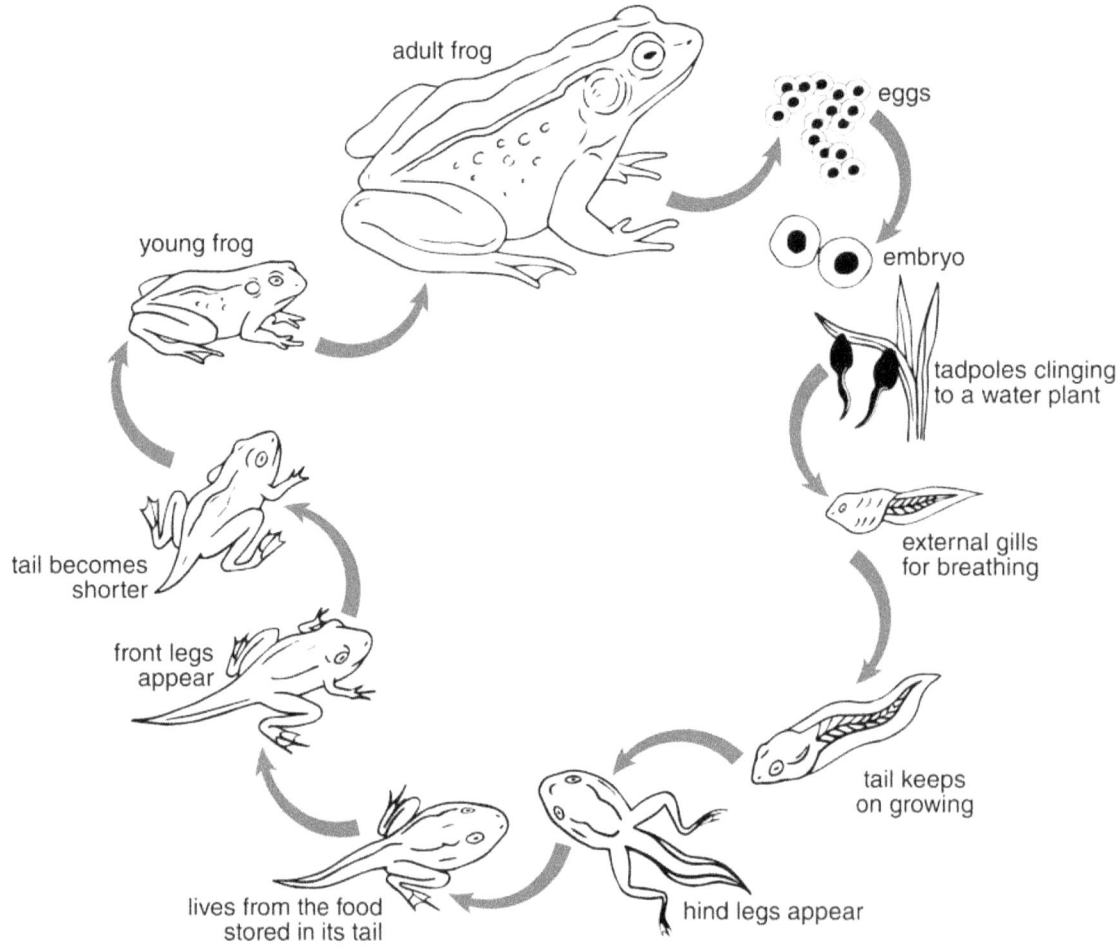

♦ **Processes** ♦

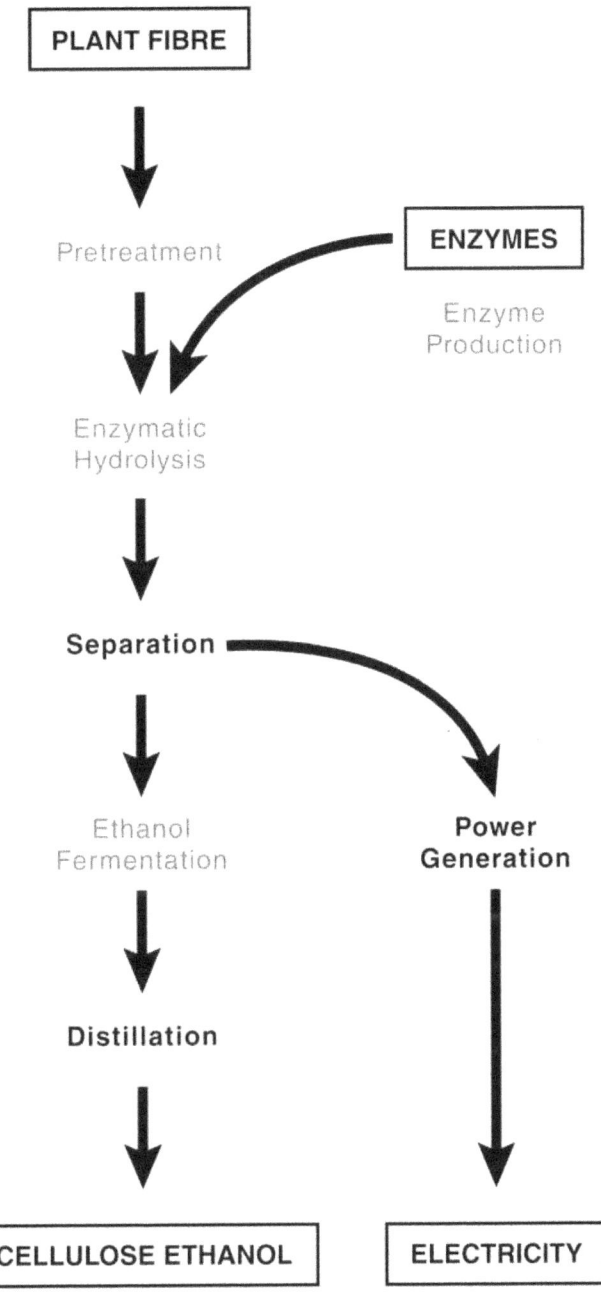

Exercise
Write an introduction, overview and main body for this process.

♦ Processes ♦

The illustration shows the different stages needed in the production of cellulose ethanol and electricity from the original ingredients of plant fibre and enzymes.

To begin with, plant fibre enters the pretreatment phase of this process with the addition of enzymes. This results in enzymatic hydrolysis where the plant fibre begins to react with the enzymes. Following this particular stage, the mixture is divided into two parts. One part is used for the production of electricity and the other part starts a stage known as ethanol fermentation. This fermentation, once complete, is then able to enter the distillation stage of the process which is then responsible for the production of cellulose ethanol as an end product.

116 words

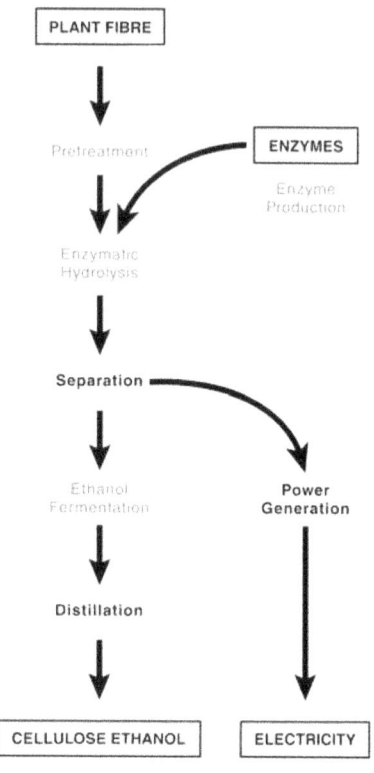

This sample report is only 116 words so far short of the minimum word requirement of 150 words meaning that the Task Achievement will be low.

One way to increase the word count is by writing a conclusion. Remember, if you write an overview in ANY Task 1 you never need to write a conclusion but this is an emergency so you could add a final paragraph as the conclusion which can summarize the whole production process. Another way is by developing a style of writing where you can make sentences longer without really saying much more than you have already. Look at the example below:

The illustration **presented here** shows the different stages needed in the production of cellulose ethanol and electricity from the original ingredients of plant fibre and enzymes.

To begin **the whole production process, the diagram clearly shows that** plant fibre **must enter** the **so-called** pretreatment phase of this process **along** with the addition of enzymes. **After some time**, this results in **the start of the second stage of the process**, enzymatic hydrolysis, where the plant fibre begins to react with the enzymes. Following this particular stage, the mixture is **then** divided into two parts. One part **of this** is used for the production of electricity and the other part starts **the third** stage known as ethanol fermentation. This fermentation, once complete, is then able to enter the **very last** stage, the distillation stage of the **production** process, which is then responsible for the production of cellulose ethanol as an end product.   **150 words**

♦ Flow Charts ♦

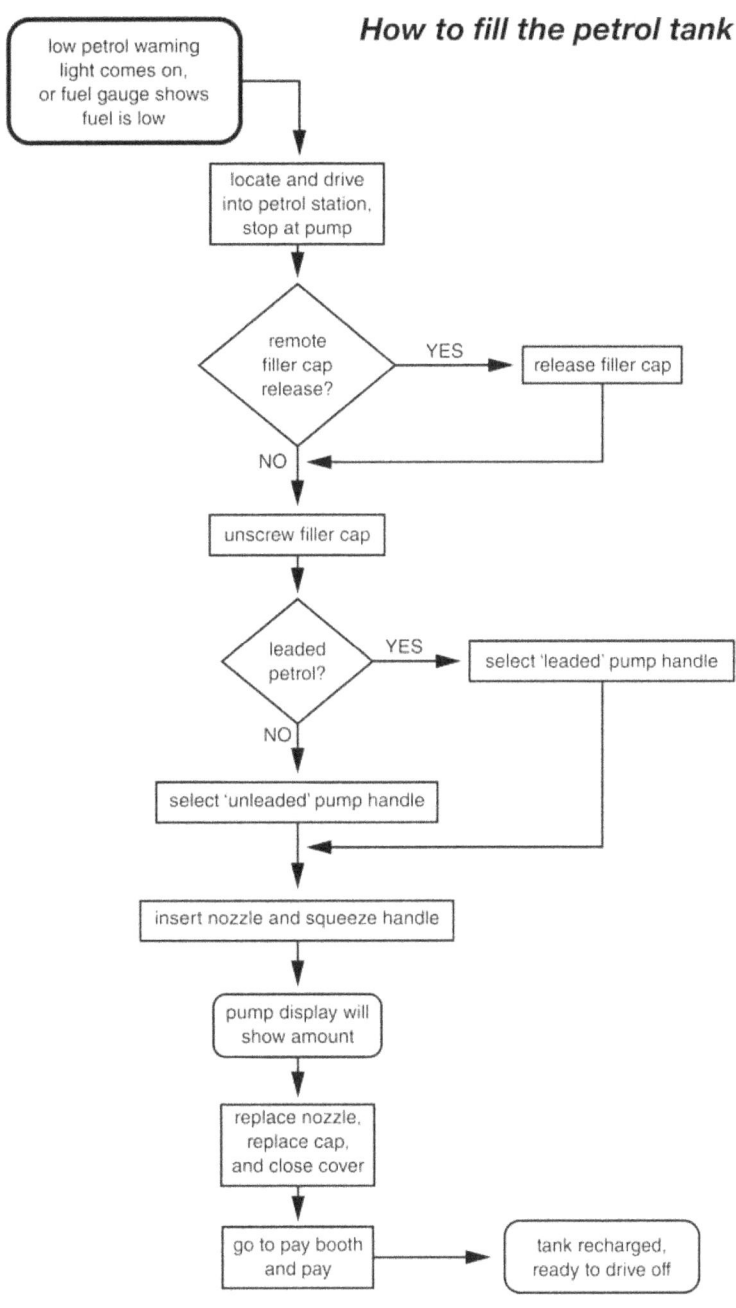

How to fill the petrol tank

Exercise
Write an introduction, overview and main body for this flow chart.

N.B. You can use simple present (active) for flow charts. Remember to use a variety of time order phrases and NEVER forget the overview (for ANY Task 1) as your Task Achievement will suffer. For flow charts it is possible to have the introduction and overview in one sentence.

♦ Flow Charts ♦

The illustration presented here highlights the various stages involved in the filling of a petrol tank from when the low petrol warning light comes on to when the petrol has been paid for and car is ready to drive off.

The first indication that the petrol tank needs to be filled is when either the warning light comes on or the fuel gauge indicates that petrol is low. This alerts the driver to find a petrol station and stop the vehicle by a petrol pump. If the cap can be released remotely this is done or it might have to be unscrewed. A choice is then made as to whether leaded or unleaded petrol. Having done this the appropriate pump handle is then selected and the nozzle inserted into the tank. The handle is then squeezed in order to allow the petrol to flow into the tank. While this is being done the amount of petrol being bought is shown on a display. Once sufficient petrol has been put into the tank the nozzle is put back onto the pump, the cap put on and the cover closed. The petrol is then paid for at the booth and then it is possible to drive away with a full tank.

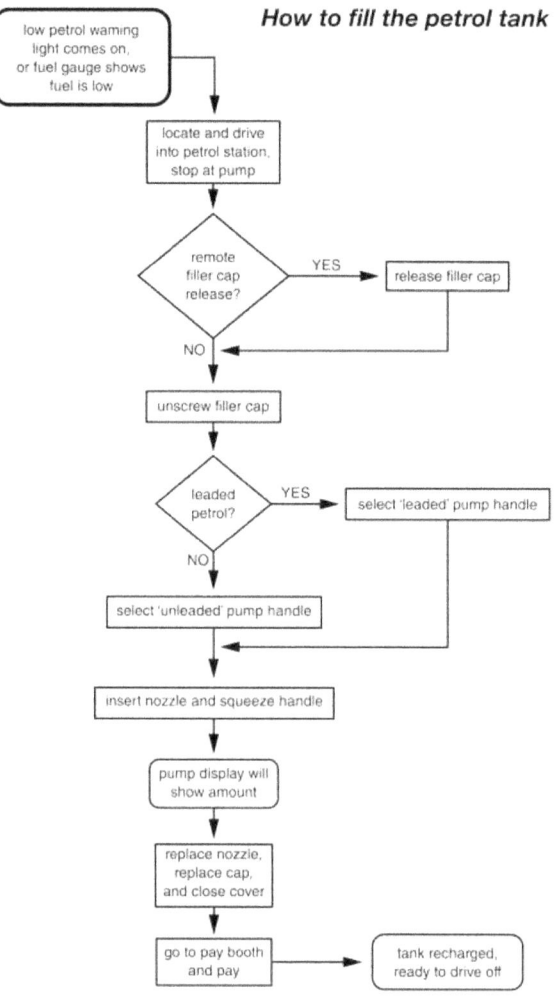

♦ **Maps** ♦

Like all of the processes, cycles and flow charts, maps are very descriptive. This means you simply write about what you see and do not need to analyze in the way you do with other Task 1 charts like bar charts and tables.

A good understanding of how to describe the location of various things is very important and so a good knowledge of prepositions is required. Also, because you are describing a map you can also use map directions

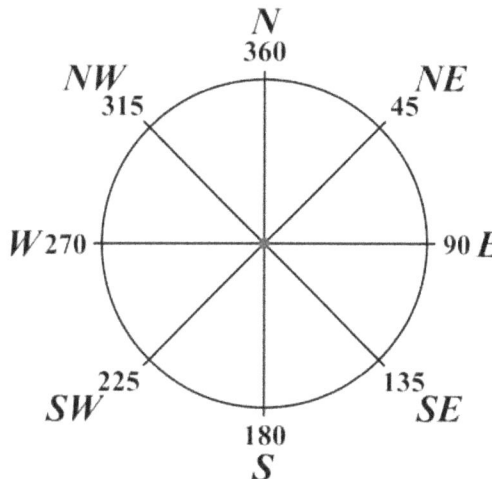

How you write these directions can vary depending on whether you are using American English or British English.

N.B. In the IELTS test you can use either spelling but it is important to maintain one style throughout. This means if you start by using the American style – **southwest** – you must not use the British English style later on – **south-west**.

	American English	British English	Alternatives
N	north	north	above
S	south	south	below
W	west	west	to the left of
E	east	east	to the right of
NW	northwest	north-west	
SW	southwest	south-west	
NE	northeast	north-east	
SE	southeast	south-east	

N.B.: These words are not usually capitalized because they are simply being used to show location within a specific region.

♦ **Maps** ♦

Try to complete the sentences in the following two exercises to help you develop these important skills.

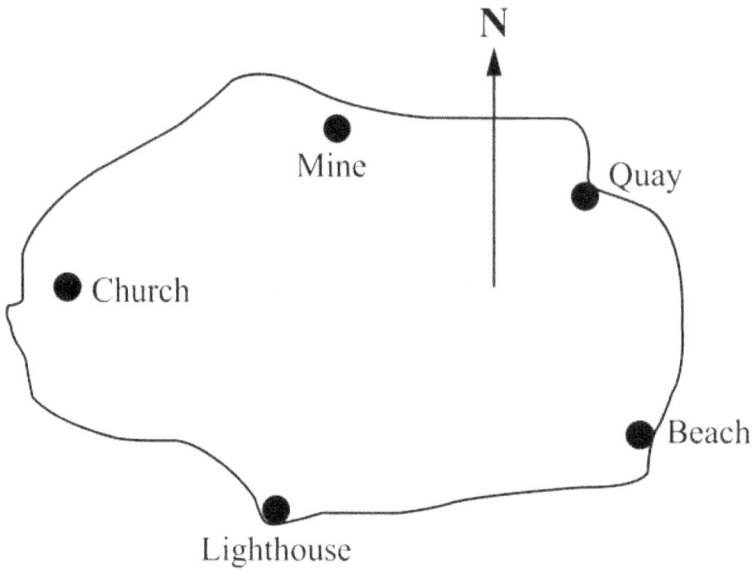

Exercise

Complete the sentences below by using the map of the island above. The tower is located where all of the lines cross.

1. The beach is to the …………… of the tower.
2. The tower is ……………….. of the church
3. The mine is ……………….. of the tower.
4. The quay is to the ……………….. of the tower.
5. The lighthouse is ……………….. of the tower.

♦ **How to write an Introduction** ♦

Like all Task 1 reports you need to write an introduction when writing maps. This is very easy and it is possible for you to use a standard phrase to start like:

The maps show the changes that occurred in ___ (place) ___ over a ___ (time period)

The maps illustrate how ___ (place) ___ has changed over a ___ (time period)

♦ Maps ♦

♦ How to write an Overview ♦

The overview simply states what the overall effect of these changes has been.

For example:

Overall, the island has seen significant changes in infrastructure over the given time period.

♦ How to write a Main Body ♦

When writing the main body it is important to remember that we do not usually know when any changes happened other than sometime within the stated time period. You do, however, need to make sure that certain changes are placed in the correct order. For example:

A hotel was built on an open space just below the golf course. The 5 trees were cut down to make room for a new hotel.

It seems more logical to write:

The 5 trees, located just below the golf course, were cut down in order to make room for a new hotel.

The selection of good verbs to describe what has happened is essential and a selection are provided below.

> **To give way to**
>
> **To make way for**
>
> **To be replaced by**
>
> **To be converted into**
>
> **To be transformed into**
>
> **To be built in place of**

♦ Maps ♦

The maps below show the changes that have taken place at the seaside resort of Templeton between 1984 and 2013.

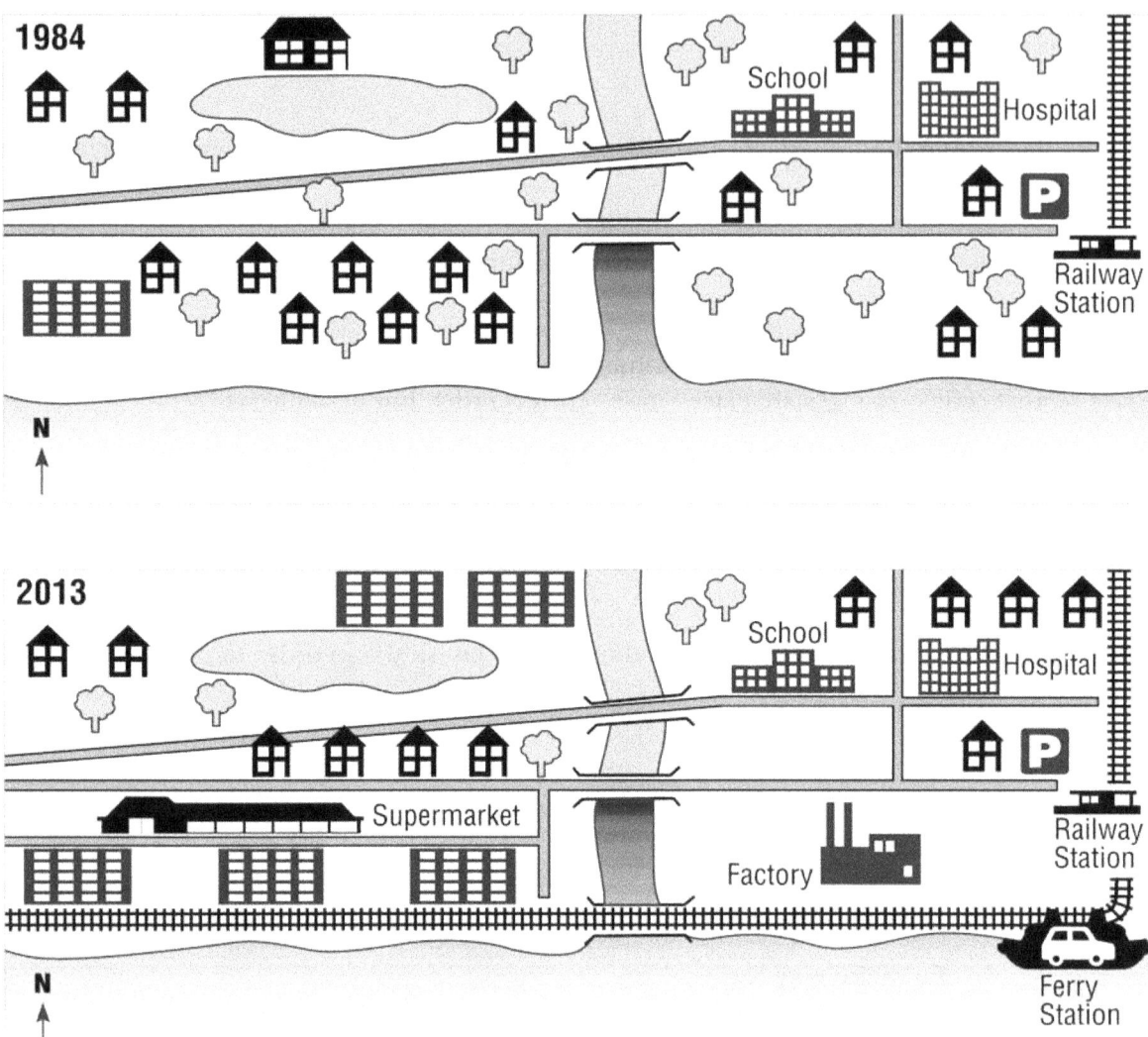

Exercise
Write an introduction, overview and main body for this map..

N.B. As stated before, there is no way of knowing when each change happened other than noting that it happened somewhere between 1984 and 2013. It would be wrong, therefore, to state, for example, **a factory was built in 2013 between the river and the railway station**. It is important to note all the changes as well as state which part of the map these places are located. You can use prepositions and map directions to do this. Typical verb tenses would be simple present and simple past (active and passive).

♦ Maps ♦

The maps below show the changes that have taken place at the seaside resort of Templeton between 1984 and 2013.

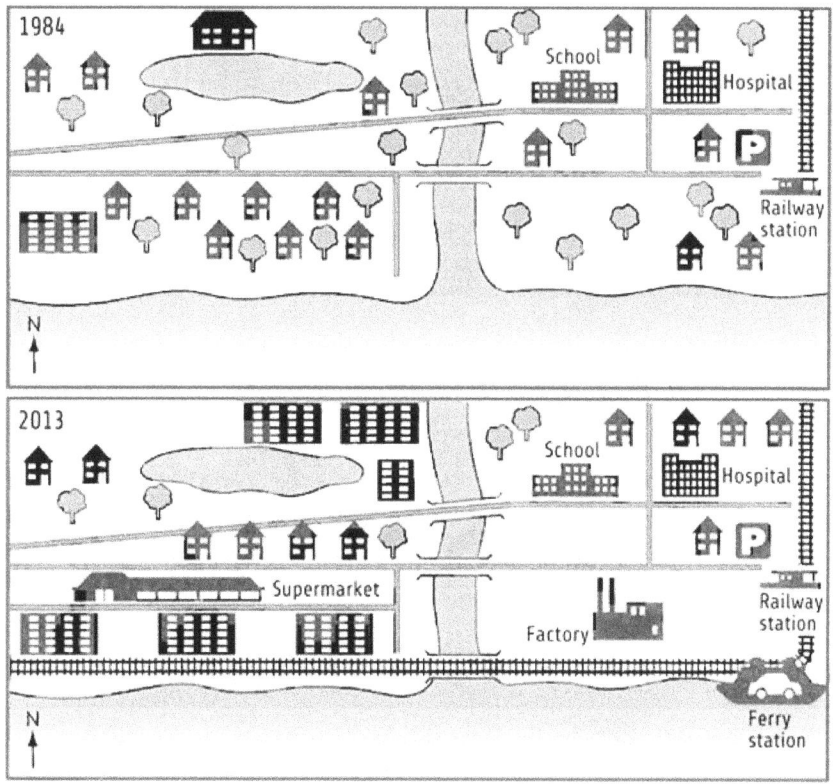

The maps show the changes that occurred in Templeton over a 29-year period form 1984 to 2013. Overall, the area has seen significant changes in infrastructure over the given time period.

The single residential building located above the lake to the west of the river **was replaced by** two large high rise buildings. The small house to the east of the river **made way for** another high rise building. To the south of the two roads and in the southwest of the map a large supermarket **was developed** along with three large high rise buildings **in place of** some other residential buildings. The school to the east of the river **remains the same** but the hospital to its right **has now got** two more smaller buildings above the main building. The railway station seen in the eastern part of the map **now has an extended railway line** heading south to a new ferry station on the coast. It then heads west past the supermarket and high rise apartments. Between the river and the railway station a factory **was built**.

45

ANSWERS

Page 3

1. The pie chart presented shows data on the number of miles travelled by 5 types of transport in 7 different countries.

2. The two tables present information on the number of crimes per 5 different age groups in 4 cities in Europe over a 4-year period form 2003 to 2006.

3. The line chart shows the number of students attending 3 different schools over an 11- year period from 2000 to 2010.

4. The bar chart presents data on the rising number of people in 6 countries over a 51-year period from 1960 - 2010.

1. The table shows information on changes in the number of people incarcerated for drugs in Brazil, Peru, and Columbia over a 4-year period from 1996 to 1999.

2. The bar chart presents data on the number of listeners of 5 radio stations over four different age groups.

3. The pie chart gives information on the annual sales of 8 consumer products in 5 European cities over a 12-year period form 2005 to 2016.

Page 4

The line chart presents data on the annual sales of cars over a 6-year period from 1997 to 2002 by two car companies called X and Y. Overall, it is clear that company Y was selling more cars than the other company in 1997 but this position was reversed by the end of this period.

Page 7

More specifically, the longest continued **rise** in festival goers was from 1976 to 1988 where figures **rose** from a little under 250 to exactly 4,000; an **increase** of just over 3,750 over 13 years. This figure was not attained again for 19 years when **more** people went to the Nelsonville Music Festival in 2006 with a total of slightly more than 4,000, more visitors than at any other time. This was an obvious contrast to 1976, the **lowest attendance** over this time. One further point to note is that attendance **remained the same** at exactly 3,000 over 3-consecutive years from 1996 to 1998. After the continued **climb** to 1988, attendance bottomed out in 1992 and 1994 with a little over 2,500 in both years.

Page 8

The bar chart compares and contrasts the changes **in** the importance **of** 10 environmental issues faced by America **over** a 4-year period from 2003 to 2006.

Overall, although the majority **of** these problems became less important over this period of time, awareness **of** the need to address global warming rose dramatically.

More specifically, the biggest change **in** importance was **for** the issue of global warming, rising **from** a little over 20% **to** just under 50%. Acid rain stayed **at** 10th place with a little under 25% in both years. Both overpopulation and ozone depletion remained unchanged **at** a little under 25.0% and 22.5% respectively. The biggest reversal in importance was **for** water pollution which was the most important environmental problem in 2003 with a little under 40%; figures fell **to** slightly under 15% to just over 25%. This compared with views **for** toxic waste which dropped from a little over 30% to a little under 22.5%.

Page 10

Verb	Noun
decreased	a decrease
fell	a fall
dropped	a drop
declined	a decline
dipped	a dip
reduced	a reduction
weakened	a weakening

Verb	Noun
increased	an increase
rose	a rise
climbed	a climb
improved	an improvement
recovered	a recovery
grew	a growth

Page 11

1. Fuel consumption **rose dramatically** from 120 litres in 2006 to 360 litres in 2007, a 3-fold rise.

2. There was **a slight drop** in average temperature between 1975 and 2005 of 0.3C.

3. Bakers experienced a steady **rise** in salary over 6-consecutive years (1963 - 1968) of 10% per year.

4. The number of online students **increased** from an initial 5 students in March to 130 in December.

5. The recycling program resulted in a **2-fold climb** in the amount of paper recycled, 600kg to 1,200kg.

Page 12

1. In 1995, Australian **exports** to South East Asia were slightly less than 30% of exports.

2. The early 80s witnessed a substantial **drop** to 500 million.

3. After 1999, there was a gradual **fall** to nearly 73 minutes in 2002, and as a result, the number of minutes of a local call in 2002 was equal to that of 1995.

4. In Italy, the ratio will show a **dramatic** increase **from** 24.1% to 42.3%.

5. Theme parks received less than 400 thousand guests, and the sports events had **slightly** less than 200 thousand.

6. The percentage of people possessing computers saw a **gradual increase** from less than 60 percent to more than 70 percent in 2010.

7. By the year 2005, gas usage experienced an **increase** from 29.63% to 30.31% whereas the extraction of petro plunged **significantly** to only 19.55%.

8. In the following period between 1989 and 1993, the number of women killed by the disease **remained** unchanged at just over 480.

9. The number of texts used was largest in the under 18 group, at **slightly** under 3,000.

10. The suburban areas suffered the **sharpest** climb in growth rate among the three areas, and jumped to 8% from 2%.

Page 13

The bar chart presents data on the number of books sold by six branches of a publishing company over two complete years, 2000 and 2001. The overall trend shows that, with one exception, sales in 2001 was higher than in 2000.

Page 15

The line chart presents data on the number of earthquakes experienced in one region over a 12-month period.

Page 17

The table shows data on global mobile phone sales for 6 named companies over two consecutive years, 2005 and 2006. Overall, Nokia had the majority of sales while BenQ Mobile had the least.

Page 19

The table gives information from a survey regarding the ratings of students for the 5 different factors that make a university special in three different years. Overall, the range of modules offered was always seen as the least important aspect but print resources always ranked as the most important.

Page 21

The table provides data comparing 10 different sectors of employment and the three different age groups employed in them. The least preferred occupation for any age group was accountancy with the youngest group favouring retail and the oldest group manufacturing.

Page 23

The table shows the changes in total deforestation in 10 countries and total changes in 62 in the periods 2000-2005 and 1990-2000. The overall trend shows that Malaysia experienced the biggest and Indonesia the smallest changes.

Page 25

1. Both Brazil and Argentina experienced the same literacy levels in 2003 with 98.2%

2. The most expensive apartments were in Hong Kong with an average weekly cost of £1,750.

3. The biggest difference in tourism occurred between Thailand and Cambodia where figures were 4.5 million and 2 million respectively; a difference of 2.5 million.

The pie chart gives information on the four different regions that food products are distributed by Company ABC. Overall, it can be clearly seen that the Caribbean is the main place food is sent and Latin America the least.

Page 27

The pie chart shows data concerning four different mobile phone companies and their market share. Overall, Android has the biggest portion of the market with other phones talking the smallest portion

Page 29

The two tables show information regarding potato consumption and production in 5 different areas around the world in 2006.

Page 33

1. The coffee is filtered **in order to** separate the grains from the coffee.

2. The seeds are crushed **before** they are boiled for 10 minutes.

Page 42

1. The beach is to the **southeast** of the tower.
2. The tower is **to the east** of the church
3. The mine is **to the northwest** of the tower.
4. The quay is to the **northeast** of the tower.
5. The lighthouse is **to the southwest** of the tower.

www.ingramcontent.com/pod-product-compliance
Lightning Source LLC
Chambersburg PA
CBHW081926170426
43200CB00014B/2845